THINGS
TO DO
NOW YOU'RE A
MOM

First published in Great Britain in
2008 by Spruce, an imprint of
Octopus Publishing Group Ltd
Carmelite House
50 Victoria Embankment
London EC4Y 0DZ
www.octopusbooks.co.uk

An Hachette UK Company
www.hachette.co.uk

The authorized representative in
the EEA is Hachette Ireland,
8 Castlecourt Centre,
Castleknock Road,
Castleknock, Dublin 15,
D15 YF6A, Ireland

This edition published in 2025
by Hamlyn

Distributed in the US by
Hachette Book Group
1290 Avenue of the Americas
4th and 5th Floors
New York, NY 10104

Distributed in Canada by
Canadian Manda Group
664 Annette St.
Toronto, Ontario,
Canada M6S 2C8

ISBN 978-0-60063-881-0

A CIP catalogue record
for this book is available
from the British Library.

Printed and bound in China

10 9 8 7 6 5 4 3 2 1

Publisher: Lucy Pessell
Designer: Dani Leigh & Isobel Platt
Editor: Feyi Oyesanya
Assistant Editor: Samina Rahman
Production Manager:
Allison Gonsalves

Picture Credits: iStock

MIX
Paper | Supporting
responsible forestry
FSC® C144853
www.fsc.org

THINGS
TO DO
NOW YOU'RE A
MOM

hamlyn

INTRODUCTION

When we give birth, we move from being women to mothers, and our worlds change in tandem with this transformation. Our eyes are opened to new sights; we see things through the eyes of our newborn babies, and we view ourselves and the world around us very differently. There are few mothers who don't stare in amazement at their babies, awestruck by the beauty and wonder of new life and the miracle of birth. In many ways, the new lives we have created provide us with new lives of our own, and we can bask in the pleasure of recreating ourselves, while giving our newborns the best possible start in life. We are the holders of their memories, their guiding stars, their source of nurturing and unconditional love, and for many, many years the most important people in their lives. This is both a responsibility and an honor, and there are few women who don't rise to the challenge of giving everything they have and are to offer their children the world.

MOM

From the sleepy hours after birth, we move into days and weeks where time loses its meaning, and the development of our babies defines our world. As they learn to focus, reach out and smile, so we learn to find our place in the world - in our new role as mothers. When they roll over, sit up, and take their first tentative steps, we cheer them on, always adapting to their changing needs and our own changing lives. We change as they do, and as we set out on this journey, we may find that we learn more about ourselves, and become more capable, more in tune with our needs as well as those of our babies. Anything and everything is possible, once you've created a new life.

This book is a treasure trove of things that, you, as a new mother, can do - a guide to inspire you as you embark upon the most rewarding adventure of your life. Having a baby may change your life, but it doesn't need to limit it. Motherhood can present the most exciting opportunity for new experiences, trying things you never knew were possible and, above all, forming a relationship with the most wonderful new friend you could ever have imagined. This book will show you how.

There's no doubt that motherhood can be tiring and challenging at times, but it is also possible to feel stimulated and energized - sharing your life in different ways, and taking the time to get to know yourself and your own needs alongside those of your growing baby. For this reason, you'll find here a bundle of ideas for activities to keep you on your toes, explore your creativity, challenge, motivate and encourage you, help you wind down, and, better still, do something outrageous - just because you can. So instead of feeling that your world has been turned upside down, turn the world on its head instead, and revel in the joy of your new life as a mom. Replace what you miss with equally stimulating pursuits. Be prepared to test yourself, and push yourself that little bit further to create the life you've always wanted. Take some time for reflection and take off your watch to enjoy the fresh innocence of your baby and the feelings that being a mother inspire in you. Find pleasure in the everyday and in the comfort of being adored by your baby. And when the feeling strikes, join together with a group of other mothers and get out there and paint the town (baby) pink or blue!

There will be days when you'll bask in serenity and cherish being at home with your baby, and times when exhaustion overwhelms you. Use these moments to restore your sense of calm, and nurture your mind and body. The very best mothers look after themselves, too, so make yourself a priority. You'll find many ways to do just that in this book.

Sing, dance, laugh, share, love and, above all, celebrate. This book is for you.

#1
MOM

'Mom', 'Mommy' or 'Mama'? Have you thought about what you would like to be called by your new baby? The origin of the word 'Mum' is Middle English, to imitate the sound made with closed lips. Welcome yourself, as a new Mom, with a gentle 'mmm'.

In Hawaiian, 'mother' is 'makuahine' and 'baby' is 'kama'. In Swahili, the word for infant is 'maliaka' and a mother is 'mzaa'. Unfamiliar words, perhaps, but still difficult to say without a smile.

It's no surprise that everything feels different. When we give birth, we are as newborn as our babies. Relish this feeling, and enjoy seeing the world with new eyes.

As a woman you are a wonder. You might not have realized it before, all moms are truly superheroes. Contemplate all the things you can do now that you've never been able to do before.

This is your special time to get to know your baby. Too many visitors can feel exhausting, so find the courage to say 'no' to acquaintances.

KEEP YOUR FACE CLOSE TO YOUR NEWBORN WHEN YOU TALK, SING AND SMILE. LET THEM GET TO KNOW YOU WITH CRYSTAL CLEAR VISION.

Being a Mom allows you to rediscover your own inner child. Relish the time spent blowing raspberries or bouncing your baby in the air. Laugh and play to your heart's content.

Cover your bed with luxurious cushions and bed linen to create an extra special place to relax, or feed your baby. Indulgence is the key word!

ENJOY SLEEPING ON YOUR TUMMY AFTER MANY MONTHS OF LIFE WITH A BUMP.

Close your eyes and marvel at the silky softness of your baby's skin as you stroke them. Nothing compares...

There is no definitive 'how to' guide or rulebook for being a mom, so learn to trust your instincts.

BREATHE IN THE MAGICAL SMELL OF A NEW BABY – COULD YOU EVER FIND THE WORDS TO DESCRIBE IT?

Don't expect too much from yourself in the early days; remember, you have just given birth, which is an achievement in itself.

Rearrange your priorities, and shorten your 'to-do' list. If you get even one thing done in the first few weeks and months, you've done well.

Sometimes motherhood can be isolating, so join a local baby group, and keep up regular conversations with old friends.

Find ways to nurture yourself after giving birth. Simple pleasures can feel extra special.

ONE OF THE BIGGEST PLEASURES IN LIFE IS SIMPLY GAZING AT YOUR SLEEPING CHILD.

Let things go a little.
Take pride in the fact
that you are doing one
of the most important
jobs in the world.

SMILE AT OTHER
MOTHERS YOU SEE, EVEN
IF YOU DON'T KNOW
THEM. THEY MIGHT BE
HAVING A DIFFICULT DAY.

**MOMS
DESERVE
THE BEST.**

If you feel overwhelmed by the sheer number of new emotions that sweep over you, take some time to let them out.

It's just fine to admit that there are some things you don't know about being a mom. Ask questions, and learn from your mistakes. No one gets it right, even second, third or fourth time round!

Babies cry to communicate something. Tune into your instincts and learn to distinguish your baby's different cries.

A SMILE RELEASES FEEL-GOOD ENDORPHINS AND IS ONE OF THE FIRST EXPRESSIONS YOUR BABY WILL MIMIC.

There are few things as precious as feeling your baby's tiny hands curling around your finger.

Don't feel guilty if it takes an hour or more to get up and dressed, and remember that there is nothing in the rulebook that says you can't spend your day in pajamas.

"Motherhood:

All love begins and ends there."

– ROBERT BROWNING

Stare out of a window as your baby feeds, and let your mind wander. Enjoy the stillness and peace.

Vacuum while your baby is sleeping. Vacuums produce something called 'white noise' which often soothes even the crankiest baby off to sleep. What's more, if they get used to background noise early on, they will learn to sleep through it.

A cup of chamomile tea is an easy, gentle way to instill a sense of calm as you find your feet as a new mom.

As a new mom, you'll need to keep your energy levels up. It's often easier to eat smaller meals, regularly throughout the day, to keep your blood sugar stable.

Remember how important you are too, even when you are giving everything for your baby. Take time to look after yourself.

With a little non-toxic fingerpaint, use your baby's handprint to create perfect thank-you cards for all the gifts you have received.

AS YOU ADJUST TO LIFE WITH YOUR NEW FRIEND, TRY TO REST OR SLEEP WHEN YOUR BABY DOES AND FIND A RHYTHM FOR THE DAY TOGETHER.

It's impossible to 'spoil' a new baby with cuddles and kisses. If 'well meaning' relatives tell you otherwise, just take a deep breath and ignore them.

Make time for your partner. Although a new baby can absorb every waking moment, there are other people who love you too.

THE HOUSE MIGHT BE
A MESS, BUT SO WHAT?
RELAX AND ENJOY YOUR
NEW DAYS AS A MOTHER.

Remember, other people
won't 'break' your baby, so
don't hesitate to hand them
over, and never be afraid to
ask for help when you need
it. Even an hour with your
hands free can present an
amazingly refreshing break.

TRY CARRYING YOUR BABY IN A SLING; THEY LOVE THE CLOSENESS OF YOUR BODY.

"The moment a child is born, the mother is also born. She never existed before. The woman existed, but the mother, never. A mother is something absolutely new."
– RAJNEESH

Marvel at your new ability to put the kettle on, brush your hair and fold the washing with one hand. Celebrate your new skills, and look down at the reason for your newfound dexterity.

Love yourself without makeup – your beauty, as a mother, is something that could never fit into a tube or bottle.

Look in the mirror and welcome your new self – now a mom – to the world. Celebrate the shape of your body.

CHERISH THE WARMTH AND GLOW OF HOLDING A BABY, EVEN LONG PAST HER BEDTIME. ENJOY EVERY MOMENT; THEY GROW UP TOO QUICKLY.

After a restless night with your baby, place cotton wool pads soaked in chamomile tea on your eyelids to soothe tired eyes.

You and your baby shared a powerful journey through labor. A trip to a cranial osteopath is a gentle way for both of you to realign and help your bodies to settle into your new life.

Use affirmations to boost your self-esteem. These are simple words of positive encouragement that, when spoken aloud, can really help to nurture a sense of calm – or get you back on track when the going is tough.

MAKE UP YOUR OWN AFFIRMATIONS FOR BEING A MOM, AND STICK THEM AROUND THE HOUSE ON NOTE CARDS.

Make time in your day to see other adults. It doesn't mean that you love your baby any less, but it can provide invaluable social interaction.

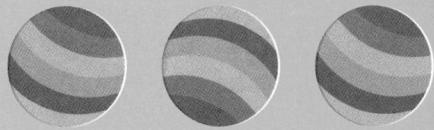

Start a toy-share scheme with other parents. Not only will you make new friends, but your baby's toys will seem forever new.

Host a 'pot luck' lunch with other new moms. If everyone brings one dish, you all get to eat without the hassle of cooking a big meal.

If you want to see the latest blockbuster, many local cinemas hold regular mother-and-baby screenings, where no one minds if there is a bit of background noise.

Get involved in a baby-sitting circle; leaving your child with another parent is an easy, cheap way to make a little time for yourself, and many other moms will love a little free time of their own, too!

NOW YOU ARE OUT OF MATERNITY CLOTHES, GO ON A SHOPPING SPREE TO FIND CLOTHES THAT FIT AND SUIT THE NEW YOU.

If you ever feel you might have the baby blues, don't be scared to chat to your doctor about getting some extra support. Sometimes just a sympathetic ear and a reassuring chat can make all the difference.

Record your baby on video regularly. It's amazing how quickly we forget the little things, and the huge changes that occur in those early weeks and years.

Make a pact with your friends to talk about things that are not baby-related at least some of the time.

Network! You may not plan to return to work, or you may have plenty of time before you even contemplate the prospect, but contacts will always come in handy.

"Nothing has a better effect upon children than praise."
– SIR PHILIP SIDNEY

To remind yourself that you can still be a mom and feel sexy.

> "The soul is healed
> by being with children."
> – FYODOR DOSTOYEVSKY

**Order a takeaway, light
some candles, put on some
smoochy music and have
a romantic 'date' at home
with your partner. Even if
it seems like hard work at
the time, you'll both enjoy
being alone together.**

MOMS NEED TO UNWIND AT THE END OF THE DAY, TOO. DON'T FEEL GUILTY ABOUT THAT BIG GLASS OF WINE.

Savor the taste of shellfish, soft cheese and all the other things that you were unable to eat while you were pregnant.

When you feel your normal sexual self again, don't forget the contraception. It is most certainly a myth that you can't get pregnant while breastfeeding!

Avoid comparing developmental stages with friend's babies; all children develop at their own pace and will do things in their own time.

Instead of thinking about all the things that you haven't done, list all the things that you have achieved. Put being a mom at the top.

Capture baby hands and feet in a clay print - one day you'll be amazed they had such teeny fingers and toes.

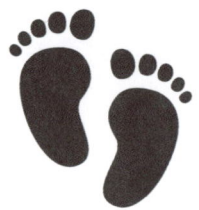

"She never quite leaves her children at home, even when she doesn't take them along."
– MARGARET CULKIN BANNING

Have a good old cry. Sometimes motherhood can be overwhelming, and your fluctuating hormones can release a flood of tears at the most amazingly unsentimental things. It's never wrong to cry, and it can provide a huge release from any tension you may be feeling.

"To describe my mother would
be to write about a hurricane
in its perfect power."
– MAYA ANGELOU

BABIES GROW SO FAST,

DON'T FEEL THAT

YOU HAVE TO BUY

EVERYTHING NEW.

"The best thing you can give children, next to good habits, are good memories."
– SYDNEY J HARRIS

One thing that being a mom teaches you is how to prioritize your time; celebrate this and never feel guilty about the things you choose to let go of.

BOOK IN FOR A FIRST AID COURSE SO YOU WON'T PANIC IF YOUR BABY EVER HAS AN ACCIDENT.

"Youth fades; love droops;
the leaves of friendship fall;
a mother's secret hope
outlives them all."
– OLIVER WENDELL HOLMES

Explore the possibilities of yoga, as it can be a great way to relax and get into shape after birth. Yoga also helps to develop your baby's coordination and awareness of her body.

"Motherhood has a very humanizing effect. Everything gets reduced to essentials."
– MERYL STREEP

Babies spend a lot of time sky-gazing, so join in! Lie back and relax as you watch clouds vaporize and float across the sky. Teach your baby to find magic in the natural world.

Find a book that shows just how much edible food there is in the countryside and head out for a walk with your baby to gather new treats.

"Children reinvent
your world for you."
– SUSAN SARANDON

YOU DO SO, SO
MUCH AS A MOTHER,
SO ACCEPT OFFERS
OF HELP WITH
GRACE AND ALLOW
OTHERS TO DO
THINGS FOR YOU.

"A little girl, asked where her home was, replied, 'where mother is'."

– KEITH L BROOKS

If you catch the time to cook a meal while your baby is sleeping, double or triple up the ingredients and freeze a few meals for another day.

"There is nothing more thrilling
in this world, I think, than having
a child that is yours, and yet
is mysteriously a stranger."
– AGATHA CHRISTIE

SMALL BABIES HAVE
NO CONCEPT OF SPACE
AND TIME – THIS IS
ONE OF THE REASONS
WHY THEY LOVE TO
PLAY PEEK-A-BOO.

Gentle tickling games encourage babies to laugh. Not only is it one of the most beautiful sounds imaginable, but you'll be helping to develop their speech, too.

"Before you were conceived I wanted you. Before you were born I loved you. Before you were here an hour I would die for you. This is the miracle of life."
– MAUREEN HAWKINS

Make your favorite cake from childhood and don't feel any guilt about eating it all in one go (with friends or without).

"Children are likely to live up to what you believe of them."
– LADY BIRD JOHNSON

MOMS NEED CUDDLES, TOO! A BIG HUG INCREASES LEVELS OF THE FEEL-GOOD HORMONE SEROTONIN IN YOUR BRAIN.

On the days when being a mom seems a little overwhelming, take a trip to the nearest beach or river. Throwing pebbles into water is a great way to release tension.

Take a walk in the country with your baby and gather natural treasures for a nature table.

It's a great way to let your child explore the multitude of textures, shapes and smells that make up the natural world.

Little ones love bright colors so, even if you aren't a natural artist, try painting bright bold patterns or swirls with poster paints on their walls or even windows.

Frame a lock or curl of your child's baby hair, or tuck it away in your memory box. Take a snip every year or so. Our children's hair may change color many times as they head towards adulthood, and it's lovely to see that transformation in concrete terms.

START COLLECTING BOARD GAMES FOR A GAMES CUPBOARD, AND TRY TO REMEMBER THE RULES FOR SOME OF YOUR OLD FAVORITES.

Relive your own childhood. Feel like a child again and kick autumn leaves high in the air or splash in big puddles.

FILL YOUR GARDEN
WITH NIGHTLIGHTS, AND
TAKE AN ENCHANTED
EVENING WALK
WITH YOUR BABY.

**Babies grow so fast; in just a
short time you'll be amazed
how tiny they were. Be sure
to capture the changes
with lots of photos.**

Writing is a brilliant way to share happy memories, and express any worries you might have as a mom. Why not keep a journal? It will remind you of all those milestones that are so easily forgotten as time passes.

"Just keep a spring in your heart and...ask yourself, 'Where's my sense of humor?'"
– MAE WEST

Being a mom doesn't mean you can't look glamorous. Even if you're staying in for the evening, get dressed up – if only for your own pleasure!

Remember that it's never too early to read to your baby – they'll love the sound of your voice, even if you are only reading your own books aloud!

Your baby loves the sound of your voice, and even early on learns speech patterns and intonation. So keep up the chatter.

Ask yourself why the sky is blue, and what rainbows are made of, in preparation for the many questions that will be coming your way in just a few years.

The word 'infant' means 'not able to speak', but that doesn't mean that you don't understand their signs and signals. Hold them and chat to them as often as you can – you'll be amazed by the feedback you get! And you'll soon learn to recognize when they're not happy, and want something else.

MOST BABIES UNDERSTAND SIMPLE GESTURES, SO INVENT YOUR OWN SIGN LANGUAGE.

Grow an aloe vera plant.
The gel from their leaves
is an excellent addition
to any natural
first-aid kit.

**It's all too easy
to lavish time and
attention on a baby
and forget yourself; try
to eat when baby eats,
even if it's only a snack.**

You've grown a baby, so try growing flowers. Plant your child's name in flowers, and watch it bloom in the spring.

Positive thoughts can work wonders when the daily grind gets you down. Remember that things might take a little longer, but you are just as capable as you ever were.

Inspirational books can
help you keep a sense
of yourself when you are
overwhelmed by motherhood.

DON'T START THINKING
ABOUT WORK BEFORE YOU
HAVE TO. YOU NEVER GET
THIS PRECIOUS TIME BACK.

Many women find that motherhood changes their perspective, and their dreams and visions alter. Remember that it's never too late to change direction.

"There is only one pretty child in the world, and every mother has it."
– CHINESE PROVERB

Life as a mother means

learning to juggle your life.

Turn it around and learn

to juggle like a clown.

SHARE THE JOY
OF MOTHERHOOD
AND PERFORM
A RANDOM ACT
OF KINDNESS.

If childcare arrangements have to be made, start early so that you get exactly what you want for your special baby. Do your homework and follow your instincts.

"Life is the first gift, love is the second, and understanding the third."
– MARGE PIERCY

BECOMING A MOTHER MOVES US CLOSER TO BELIEVING THAT NOTHING IS IMPOSSIBLE, AND THAT THE WORLD IS FULL OF NEW POSSIBILITIES.

Even though you might feel tired, physical activity can help you to feel re-energized. Wrap up baby and take a brisk walk, or just meander in the park for a few hours to get your blood going.

"Making the decision to have a child – it's momentous. It is to decide forever to have your heart go walking around outside your body."
– ELIZABETH STONE

You'll find you have a fierce new protective instinct, and that you'd fight tooth and nail for your little one.

Read up on common childhood ailments so you feel fully prepared when you need to care for a sick baby.

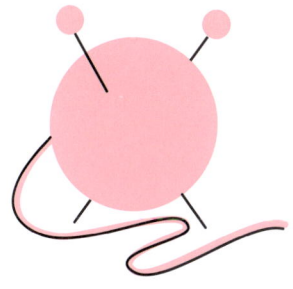

Learn to knit – it's a great way to create really special baby clothes and gives you a practical reason to sit down and relax.

How many nursery rhymes or songs from your own childhood can you remember now that you want to sing them to your child? Nursery songs are a great way to encourage a child's vocabulary and memory, and also to inspire a love of music.

BABIES HAVE A HUGE REPERTOIRE OF EXPRESSIONS. HAVE FUN MIMICKING THEM, AS THEY WILL OFTEN FIND THIS HILARIOUS.

Make some noise with a 'baby band'. Pull out pots and pans from the kitchen cupboards and bash away with wooden spoons!

"There are two lasting bequests we can give our children. One is roots. The other is wings."
– HODDING CARTER, JR

You are perfect just as you are, so avoid the temptation to compare your achievements with anyone else's. The same goes for baby. All little ones develop at different paces, and your baby will be perfect just the way they are.

YOU MIGHT VIEW YOUR PARENTS IN A NEW LIGHT NOW THAT YOU'RE A MOM.

Try to learn more about your family and its history – one day your baby will love to know where they came from.

Ask your parents to share memories of you as a baby, and take the opportunity to look through old childhood photos. Is your baby like you in more ways than one?

Make a list of the things that provide you with the most vivid memories, and try to recreate them for your own baby. Give your child something special to remember as well.

YOU'LL NEVER FORGET YOUR FIRST MOTHER'S DAY.

Memories of special days with your new baby can be kept forever. Gather mementoes of your adventures together in a scrapbook and label them.

Even if you are not religious, holding a naming ceremony for your baby is a wonderful way to welcome them to the world.

A first birthday is a milestone to celebrate, but you might also feel surprisingly emotional. Try not to fight these bittersweet emotions and take a moment in the day for reflection.

Small children love the glow of candlelight, so carve a pumpkin for Halloween and share the magic flicker of the lantern with the lights turned off.

INDULGE IN CHILDHOOD
MEMORIES AND TOAST
MARSHMALLOWS
OVER A FIRE.

Start some new family
traditions now that
you're a mom – perhaps
Father Christmas prefers
to be left a glass of wine
rather than milk!

The world seems very big when you are very small. Remember this when you talk to children, and bend down so that you can talk to them face to face.

Know when to listen and when to disregard the 'good advice' that people may send your way. The best moms blend instinct with common sense.

There is often a magical bond between the very old and the very young – watching this interaction between generations can be a moving experience.

Each place that you visit as a mom will seem forever new if you learn to view your surroundings with the wonder of a child.

Hold a seashell to your baby's ear so they can hear the sound of the sea.

GET YOUR BABY'S FIRST PASSPORT AS EARLY AS YOU CAN. YOU NEVER KNOW WHEN THE URGE TO TAKE OFF MIGHT STRIKE YOU.

Days out can be cheap and rewarding. Borrow, hire or buy a bike with a child's seat and peddle out for the day on an adventure of your choosing.

Walk barefoot in the sand with a newly toddling baby.

Go beachcombing and use the treasures you find to make a mobile or a picture frame for your child's room.

REVISIT THE PLACES YOU REMEMBER HAVING THE HAPPIEST HOLIDAYS WHEN YOU WERE A CHILD.

Keep old bread for feeding ducks. It's one of the simplest pleasures to share with a baby.

Find a 'secret' place behind a chair or under a blanket for telling magical stories and building a sense of adventure with your baby.

Live out fairy tales with your baby – visit castles, forests and palaces, and make up stories as you go.

DISCOVER THE STAIRS TOGETHER, SHUFFLING UP AND DOWN THE STEPS WITH YOUR CHILD.

What smells evoke your childhood? It might be fun to spend a day seeking them out. Play dough, crayons, gingerbread and even a summer garden might bring memories flooding back and create new ones for your baby.

WRITE YOUR VERY OWN LIST OF THINGS YOU'D LIKE TO DO NOW THAT YOU'RE...A MOM.

Join a library and see if you can find the books that you loved as a child, then share the pleasure of your memories as you read them together.

LEARNING HOW TO BE A PLAYMATE MIGHT TAKE TIME. ENJOY A DAY BEING SILLY – LET GO, GET MESSY AND GET LOST IN YOUR CHILD'S LAUGHTER.

Bring your house to life!
Play with your child
and pretend that the
stairs are a mountain,
the sofa is a boat, and
the table is a castle.

Gather leaves and
flowers that you
don't recognize, and
look them up with
an older child.

Think back to the things you really wanted to do as a child but never quite managed. Now's the time to reclaim your childhood and take your child down memory lane.

Rediscover the power of imagination and lose yourself in make-believe games – spend a day looking for fairies or chasing dragons.

Remind yourself how to use a wooden sword and a fairy wand, and prepare for the honor of being your child's first playmate.

You don't need expensive toys to have fun with your child. Rediscovering the pleasures of simple games like 'hide and seek', 'eye spy', or even 'it'.

If your child has an imaginary friend, remain interested and ask questions rather than dismissing them – the power of make-believe is a beautiful thing.

LET YOUR CHILD LOOSE WITH A BOX OF FACE PAINTS AND HAVE FUN BEING WHOEVER OR WHATEVER THEY WANT YOU TO BE FOR THE DAY.

Start collecting buttons, bows, ribbons, paper and shiny things for impromptu art sessions. Salvage boxes from recycling and have fun junk-modeling.

Transform your house or garden into a magical playground and organize a treasure hunt with a small toy as the prize at the end.

Every now and then remind your child that you have a sense of humor and 'break' an everyday rule. Why not try dancing on the table or starting a food fight?

Try reading a range of children's stories so that you can share thoughts and ideas about what they are reading.

If you have had a disagreement with your child, leave a note on their pillow telling them how much you care.

EVEN IF YOUR CHILD PRETENDS NOT TO CARE, THEY DO LOOK UP TO YOU.

Even when your child leaves home, they will cherish small gifts and mementoes that remind them of the time they spent growing up with you.

STOP – OFTEN – TO CONGRATULATE YOURSELF AND CELEBRATE YOUR ACHIEVEMENTS AS A MOM.